KISS ME, KATE

301-481-9913

Music and Lyrics by

COLE PORTER

Weston Rey
11:30
2401 VA AV

Book by

SAM and BELLA SPEWACK

Parking ent.
on 24th

based on William Shakespeare's
"The Taming Of The Shrew"

Vocal Score

1. OVMG. M, 233
2. Finale M. 61
3. # 15 110 – end

Piano Reduction by
Robert H. Noeltner

KISS ME, KATE

Produced by SAINT SUBBER and LEMUEL AYERS

First performance December 30, 1948 at the New Century Theatre, New York

Directed by JOHN C. WILSON

Choreography by Hanya Holm
Settings and Costumes by Lemuel Ayers
Musical Director Pembroke Davenport
Orchestrations by Robert Russell Bennett
Incidental Ballet Music Arranged by Genevieve Pitot

Cast of Characters

(In order of appearance)

FRED GRAHAM	Alfred Drake
HARRY TREVOR	Thomas Hoier
LOIS LANE	Lisa Kirk
RALPH	Don Mayo
LILLI VANESSI	Patricia Morison
HATTIE	Annabelle Hill
PAUL	Lorenzo Fuller
BILL CALHOUN	Harold Lang
FIRST MAN	Harry Clark
SECOND MAN	Jack Diamond
STAGE DOORMAN	Dan Brennan
HARRISON HOWELL	Denis Green
SPECIALTY DANCERS	Fred Davis, Eddie Sledge

"Taming Of The Shrew" Players

BIANCA	Lisa Kirk
BAPTISTA	Thomas Hoier
GREMIO	Edwin Clay
HORTENSIO	Charles Wood
LUCENTIO	Harold Lang
KATHARINE	Patricia Morison
PETRUCHIO	Alfred Drake
HABERDASHER	John Castello

SINGING ENSEMBLE: Peggy Ferris, Florence Gault, Joan Kibrig, Gay Laurence, Ethel Madsen, Helen Rice, Matilda Strazza, Tom Bole, George Cassidy, Herb Fields, Noel Gordon, Allan Lowell, Stan Rose, Charles Wood

DANCING ENSEMBLE: Ann Dunbar, Shirley Eckl, Jean Houloose, Doreen Oswald, Ingrid Secretan, Gissela Svetlik, Jean Tachau, Mark Breaux, John Castello, Victor Duntiere, Tom Hansen, Paul Olsen, Glen Tetley, Rudy Tone

KISS ME, KATE

Synopsis of Scenes

ACT I

SCENE 1: Stage of the Ford Theatre, Baltimore.
SCENE 2: The corridor, backstage.
SCENE 3: Dressing rooms of Lilli Vanessi and Fred Graham.
SCENE 4: Padua.
SCENE 5: Street scene, Padua.
SCENE 6: Backstage.
SCENE 7: Dressing rooms of Lilli Vanessi and Fred Graham.
SCENE 8: The church.

ACT II

SCENE 1: The stage door alley.
SCENE 2: Before the curtain.
SCENE 3: Petruchio's house.
SCENE 4: The corridor, backstage.
SCENE 5: Dressing rooms of Lilli Vanessi and Fred Graham.
SCENE 6: The corridor, backstage.
SCENE 7: Before the safety curtain.
SCENE 8: Baptista's home.

Instrumentation

Woodwind No. 1: Clarinet/Alto Saxophone/Flute
No. 2: Clarinet/Alto Saxophone/Bass Clarinet
No. 3: Clarinet/Tenor Saxophone/Oboe/English Horn
No. 4: Clarinet/Tenor Saxophone/Flute/Piccolo
No. 5: Clarinet/Baritone Saxophone/Bassoon

French Horn, 3 Trumpets, Trombone, Percussion
Harp, Piano/Celesta, Guitar/Mandolin
Violins I-II, Viola, 'Cello, Bass

Musical Program

ACT I

ACT II

KISS ME, KATE

COLE PORTER

Overture

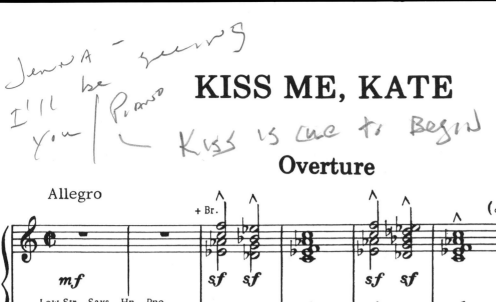

+ Bar.
cresc.
Slower (in 4)
33
Hp.
Pno.
Vlns.
L.H.
Br. tacet
Saxs.
Cello
Bells, Tpts. muted
41
Vlns.
8va
Tpts., Saxs.
Vlns., Vla.
Alto, Bar.
Hn., Cello, Tenor

Tpts.
+ Br.
49
Hp., Saxs.
(Br. sust.)
57
Vlns. + 8va
Tpts., Saxs.
f
63
Str., W. W.
+ Hn.
Br.
Saxs., Str.
rall.

69 Valse Viennoise
sf
Br., Str.
Saxs., Hn., Trb., Str.
+ Tpts.
Br., Str.
Hns., Saxs.
mf
+Bar., Trb.
77
Tutti
+ Hp.
+ Hp.
+Hp.
Hn.
+ Hp.
85
mf
Picc.
Cl.
Hp. gliss
Cym.
Hn.
mp
Saxs., Str., Hns. (Br. cued)
93
+Xyl.
etc.

* Orch. parts retain Ab signature.

etc.
mf
Hp. gliss.
(8va) Hn., Hp.
Str.
Br.
141
Cl., Ten.
(simile)
Cl.
Hn.
cresc.
etc.
+Cl., Ten., Vla.
+ Hn.
rit.
153
Moderato (always with great warmth)
Hp., muted Trpts.
Hn., Trb.

161
Tpts.
Cello,
Hn. 8va
Hn.
169
Str., W.W.
Tpts., div.
Hn., Trb.
Br. Soli
177
Str.
f passionately
Cym.
Tpts. 8va
etc.
Vln. 8va
185
Hn., Cl.
Ten.
dim.

Str., Hn.
+ Br.
+Br.
193
Hp. ad lib.
simile
199 Allegretto
Cl., Str.
tr
Cym.
Tutti
f marc.
Pno. Solo
Hp.
8va
Cym.
Trb. Solo
mf
203
Vlns. 8va
Vlns. 8va
Trb. + W. W.
Cls.
etc.
Pno. Solo
211
Vlns. 8va
+Cls. low Str.
Str. pizz.
f

219
+Tpts.
+ W. Bl. (Br. cue)
+Tpts.
Cym.
p
Trb., Hn.
Hp., Vlns. 8va
+Tpts.
Hp., Vlns. 8va
Trb. + W. W.
Pno. Solo
Cls. 8va
f
Hn. Br.
Vlns.
+ Shuffle Rhythm
233
Vivo
Br., Str. Hn.
p (+Sn. Dr. roll)

+ Saxs.
cresc.
+Trb., Cello
249
Maestoso
Vlns.
(Vlns. 8va)
f
(Tpts.)
8va
255
Vivo
+ Br.
Str.
ff
+Hns., Saxs.
+Br.
repeat ad lib until cut off
Tutti
+B♭ Timp.
Stop
Orchestra director speaks: "Is that O.K. Fred?"
263
Optional ending
+ Timp. roll al fine.
(267)

Is That all Right Mr. — Graham
Do my best Mr. Graham

No.1 Another Op'nin', Another Show

cue: FRED: How about a little smile, Miss Vanessi?
Bob

Very lively *(under dialogue)*

Hp. gliss.
33
Cello
Hp. gliss.
(end of dialogue)
41 ....FRED: That's all, thank you.
Hp. gliss.
Hn., B. Cl.
+ muted Br.
Hn., B. Cl.
HATTIE:
49
An - oth - er op' - nin', An - oth - er show, In
+Bells, Fl.
Str. Hp.
W.W.
fz
pp
Cello (Rhythm)
Hn. Trb.
Bs. pizz.

57
Phil - ly, Bos - ton, or Bal - ti - mo'e. A chance for stage
W. W.
folks to say "hel - lo" An - oth - er op - nin' of
Cls.
Str.
Hn., Trb.
65
an - oth - er show. An - oth - er job that you hope, at last,
+Cello
Br. muted
Will make your fu - ture for - get your past. An-
Cl., Hn.

73
oth - er pain where the ul - cers grow, An - oth - er op'-
W.W.
Str.
81
nin' of an - oth - er show! Four weeks you re -
Vlns.
W.W., Hp.
Hn., Hp.
hearse and re - hearse. Three weeks and it could-n't be worse.
Hp.
Vlns.
Vla.
B.Cl.
Hn., Hp.
89
One week, will it ev - er be right? Then
W. W., Hp.
B. Cl.
+Br.
sf
Cym.

97
out of the hat — it's that big first night! — The o - ver-ture
Fl., Hp.
Cls.
Str.
Str. sust.
Cello (+ Rhythm)
Bs. pizz.
— is a - bout to start. — You cross your fin - gers and
Br.
Hn.
105
hold your heart. — It's cur - tain time — and a - way we go. —
Br.
T. Saxs.
+Saxs.
HATTIE and CHORUS:
— An - oth - er op' - nin' of an - oth - er show. An -
Saxs.
Str.
Tutti
fz

113
Hp.
oth - er op' - nin', an - oth - er show In Phil - ly, Bos-
Br., Saxs.
mf
Cello
Hn.
+Str.
121
ton or Balt - i - mo'e, A chance for stage - folks to
+Str.
say "Hel-lo" An - oth - er op' - nin' of an - oth - er
Hp.
Str., Br., Rhythm
(W.W. sust.)
129
show. An - oth - er job that you hope, at last, Will
Cym.
Saxs.
Hn.

132
make your fu - ture for - get your past, — An - oth - er pain — where the
Str.
ul - cers grow, — An - oth - er op' - nin' of an - oth - er show!
Str.
B. D. Solo
145
+Vlns., Br., Saxs.
Four weeks, — you re - hearse and re - hearse, — Three weeks, —
Hn.
Hp. gliss.
Cls., Vla cello
Hp. gliss.
Cls.
153
— and it could-n't be worse, One week, — will it

Segue as one to No. 1a (dance)

cut

No.1a Another Op'nin', Another Show -Dance

29
W. W. . . . . . .
W. W. . . . . . .
W. W.
Br.
Br.
(8va)
Br.
Trb. Solo
37
W. W. div.
45
+Tpts., Hn.
W. W., Str.
sfz

53
W. W. 8va
Br., Hn.
+W. W.
Br. tacet
+Br.
61
W. W. . . . . .
(+Str. sust.)
Tutti
W. W., Str.
Cym.
gliss.
Hp., Pno.
+B. D.
Waltz
69
Str., W. W.
Cello, Tenor
etc.
W. W.
+Br.
gliss.
77
Br.

85
Br.
Vlns., Cls.
(Br. tacet)
+Br.
(Br. sust.)
fp
Cello, Hn.
Tenor
+Fl.
fp
93
fp
f
W. W.
Br.
101
Fl., Vlns.
Cl. Solo
sfz
p
f
Muted Br. sust.
(+Hp. gliss.)
(Quasi boogie)
All W. W.
8va

109
8
Br., Pno.
(+Br.8 bassa)
Cl. (or Sax.)
sfz
ff (corny)
Br., W. W.
117
Hp. gliss.
Str.
Br.
fp
W. W.
+Br.
mp
ff
W. W.
Str.
+Br.
125
Br.
Hn., Pno., Saxs., Str.
Tpt.
Trb. Soli
133
Saxs.
Vlns.
Hp. gliss.
Hp. gliss.
+B. D.

141
Hp. gliss.
+Br., Str.
ff
Br., W. W.
fz
Hp. gliss.
149
W. W.
+Br.
fp
Str. tr.
ff
W. W.
157
Str.
Br.
Br., Hn., Pno.
Saxs., Str.
W. W., Str.
sfz

165
Str.
tr
pp Br., Hn.
poco a poco cresc.
173
sempre cresc.
ff
sf
Hp., Pno.
gliss.
181
Br., Hn., Cl.
ff Saxs., Vlns.
Low Str., Trb., Pno.

+Saxs.
189
W. W.
Blues tempo (in 4)
mf
Str. Rhythm
197
fz
Hp. gliss.

205
A tempo (in 2)
W. W., Str.
ff
Tpts. 8 bassa
simile
gliss.
213
gliss.
Br.
(+Hp.)
sfz

No.1b Reprise: Another Op'nin', Another Show

cut to 19

19
HATTIE and CHORUS:
Hp.
out of the hat it's that big first night! The o - ver-ture
Cls.
(Str. sust.)
Saxs.
p
Hn.
is a - bout to start, You cross your fin - gers and
+Str. 8va
27
hold your heart, It's cur - tain time and a - way we go,
+W. W., Vlns.
35
Str. trem.
An - oth - er op' - nin', Just an - oth - er op' - nin' of an - oth -
Hp.
f
cresc.
+W. W.
ff
Trb., Hn.
Cello, Bs.

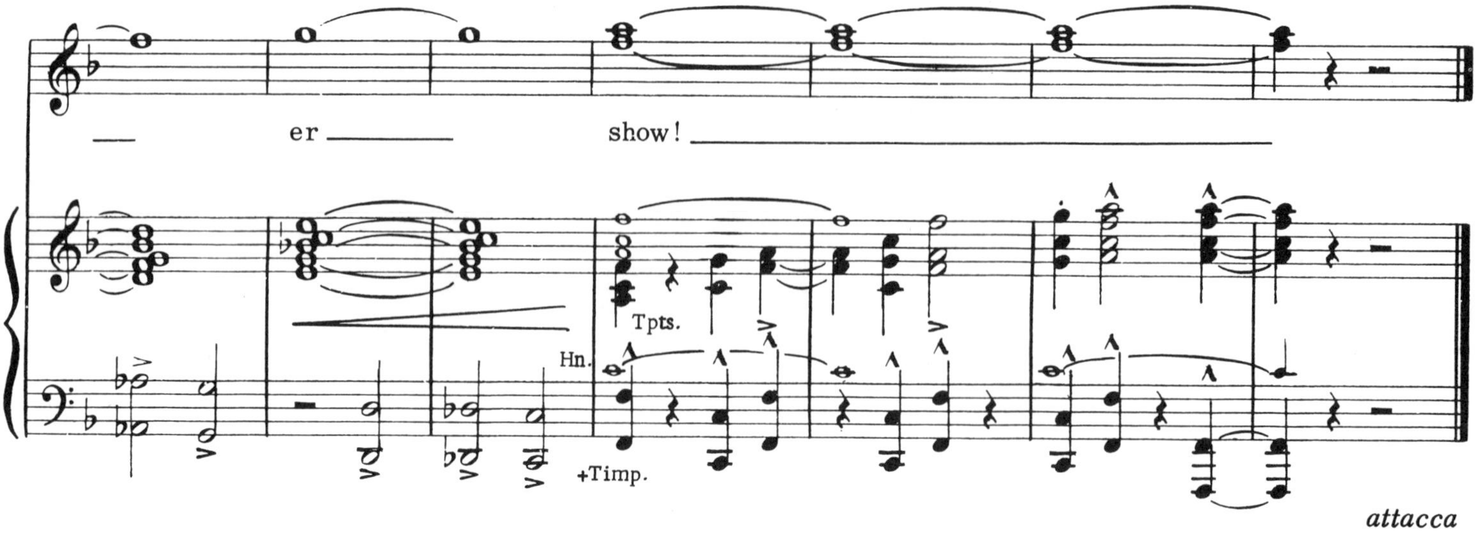

No.1c

Scene Change

(Another Op'nin', Another Show)

No. 2 Why Can't You Behave?

cue: LOIS: I'll never forgive you. Star on Broadway

19
Why can't you be good? - Tpts., Hp. And
Str.
Cls.
+Trb.
Cls., Vla.
p
do just as you should? Won't you
etc.
Cls., Trb.
Tpts., Hp.
Cls., Vla.
f
Vlns.
p
27
turn that new leaf o - ver, So your ba - by can be your slave? Oh,
Vlns.
Str., Cls.
p
why can't you be - have? There's a
+Muted Br.
Low Str.

35
farm I know near my old home town
Where we
Vlns.
Tpts., Hp., Vlns.
Br., Cls.
mp
p
Low Str.
two can go and try set-tlin' down.
There I'll
mf
mf
p
43 Slowly
a tempo
care for you for-ev-er, 'Cause you're all in the world I crave, But
Solo Vln.
Celesta
ad lib. cadenza
Cls.
Br.
Str., Hp.
Br.
f
(LOIS)
51
why can't you be-have? I al-ways
BILL
Gee, I need you kid
Vlns.
+8va
Br.
Cls., Str.
Str., Cls.
espressivo

No.2a Change of Scene

No.3 Wunderbar

cue: LILLI: No, dear. We were both in the Chorus!

29
fav - 'rite star a - bove;
What a bright - shin - ing
+Ob.
mf
molto rit.
Like our love, it's Wun - der - bar!
molto rit.
star! Like our love, it's Wun - der - bar!
p molto rit.
Hp. Solo
6
37 VERSE
FRED:
LILLI:
Gaz - ing down on the Jung - frau From our se - cret
a tempo
Hp.
Cello
Str., Pno.

45
FRED:
LILLI
cha - let for two,
Let us drink, Lieb-chen mein,
In the moon-light be-
Str., Cls.
Fl.
Hp. arpeg.
poco rit.
a tempo
nign,
To the joy of our dream come true.
To the joy of our dream come true.
W. W., Tpt. 3, Trb., Bells
Harp arpeg.
Hn.
Str.
55
REFRAIN
Wun - der - bar,
Wun - der - bar!
What a
Str., Tpts. muted
Fl.
Cello, Bsn.
+Hn.
Vln., Ob.
(8va)
(Br. tacet)

Fl.
Hn.
63
Here am I,
Fl.
per - fect night for love,
Str. div.
mf
Cello
Cls.,
Bsn.
here you are,
etc.
Br.
Why, it's tru - ly Wun - der -
Hp.
71
Hn.
Wun - der - bar, Wun - der - bar!
bar! Wun - der - bar, Wun - der - bar! We're a-
Fl.
p
Str., W. W.

Fl.
79
Not a cloud near or
lone and hand in glove,
Fl.
Str. div.
mf
Cello, Bsn., Cl.
far,
Say you
Why, it's more than Wun - der - bar!
col 8va
Hp.
Ob., Bsn., Hn.
87
A little brighter
care, dear,
Say you long, dear,
For you mad - ly.
For your
Fl., Str.
W. W., Tpts.

95
Do you swear, dear?
Fl., Str.
kiss.
Darling, gladly,
cresc.
103
Tempo I
Hp.
Life's divine, dear,
Wunderbar,
And you're mine, dear! Wunderbar,
Vlns., Vla.
W. W.. Str.
f
subito p e rit. molto
mp a tempo
Str. div.
Br., rhythm
(+Timp.)
Wunderbar!
Wunderbar!
There's our fav'rite star above.
Col 8va
Br.

111
molto rit.
What a bright shin - ing star! Like our love it's
molto rit.
Like our love it's
Col 8va
mf
(+Hn.)
Br.
p molto rit.
Hp. arpeg.
119
Both waltz
Wun - der - bar!
Wun - der - bar!
Br. Str.
f a tempo
Hn., Cello, Bsn.
127
cresc.
W.W.
f

LILLI:
135
a tempo
Wun - der - bar, Wun - der - bar!
FRED:
molto rit.
a tempo
And you're mine dear! Wun - der - bar, Wun - der - bar!
Vlns., Vla.
Str. only
subito p e molto rit.
mp
a tempo
(Br. tacet to end)
143
What a bright -
There's our fav - 'rite star a - bove. What a bright -
molto rit.
shin - ing star! Like our love, it's Wun - der - bar!
molto rit.
shin - ing star! Like our love, it's Wun - der - bar!
molto rit.
+W.W.

No.4 So In Love

cue: LILLI: My wedding bouquet.

Andante
HATTIE: I'll get you some coffee.
Piano
pp
Muted Str. (under dialogue)
(Bs. tacet)
5
LILLI:
Strange, dear, but true dear, When
L. H.
Fl., Cl.
L. H.
Fl., B. Cl.
Str.
p
(+Hp. rhythm)
+Bs.
I'm close to you, dear, The
(Fl., Cl. 8va)
(8va)
13
stars fill the sky, So in
Fl., Cl.
(+W. W. sust.)
B. Cl.

Str.
love with you am I.
W. W.
21
Solo Vln.
E - ven with - out you, My
Low W. W., Cello
(Cls. sust.)
Fl. 8va
arms fold a - bout you. You
29
(col 8va)
know, dar - ling, why, So in
Fl. (loco)
mf

love with you am I. In
37
Tpts. muted
love with the night mys - te - ri - ous, The
Cls.
Solo Vln.
più espres.
Hn., Cello
night when you first were there. In
Solo Vln.
45
Br.
love with my joy de - lir - i - ous, When I
Str., Fl.
Solo Vln.

Str.
knew that you tr could care. So
W. W.
53
Cel.
taunt me, and hurt me, De -
L. H. Cls.
L. H. Cls.
Str.
Trb.
Cls. sust.
ceive me, de - sert me. I'm
Fl., Cl. 8va
3
3
61
yours 'til I die, So in
Tpts.
Hp., Vla.
Hn.

69
love, So in love, So in love with
Cel., Fl. Solo Vln.
Solo Vln., Fl., Cel.
Cls. sust. (Tpts. tacet)
Hn.
Appassionato
you, my love, am I.
f
Tpts., Hn. Str., Cls., Hp.
77 Lilli moves about the stage
+E. H.
Fl., Celesta
Tutti
Solo Vln.
Hp.
p

(+Opt. Celesta)
espressivo
Str. trem.
Hp.
E. H. Solo
(+Bs. pizz.)
LILLI:
Solo Vln.
So,
(E. H.)
p
Str.
93
Cel.
etc. (as before)
Tpts.
taunt me, and hurt me, De -
L. H.
L. H.
ceive me, de - sert me. I'm
Fl., Cl. 8va
3
3

101
yours 'til I die, So in
love, So in love, So in love with
you, my love, am I.
109
Solo Vln.
Hn., Vln., B.Cl.
Fl., Vln., Cel.
Str., W. W.
W. W., Bells, Cel.
Trb.
Hp., Cello
+Str.
W. W., Bells, Cel.
Tpts., Str. 8va
(W. W. tacet)
Bells, Cel.
Pizz.

Cut to m. 35 (?)

No. 5 Padua Street Scene-We Open In Venice

cue: FRED: You will, my sweet, you will.

Start here

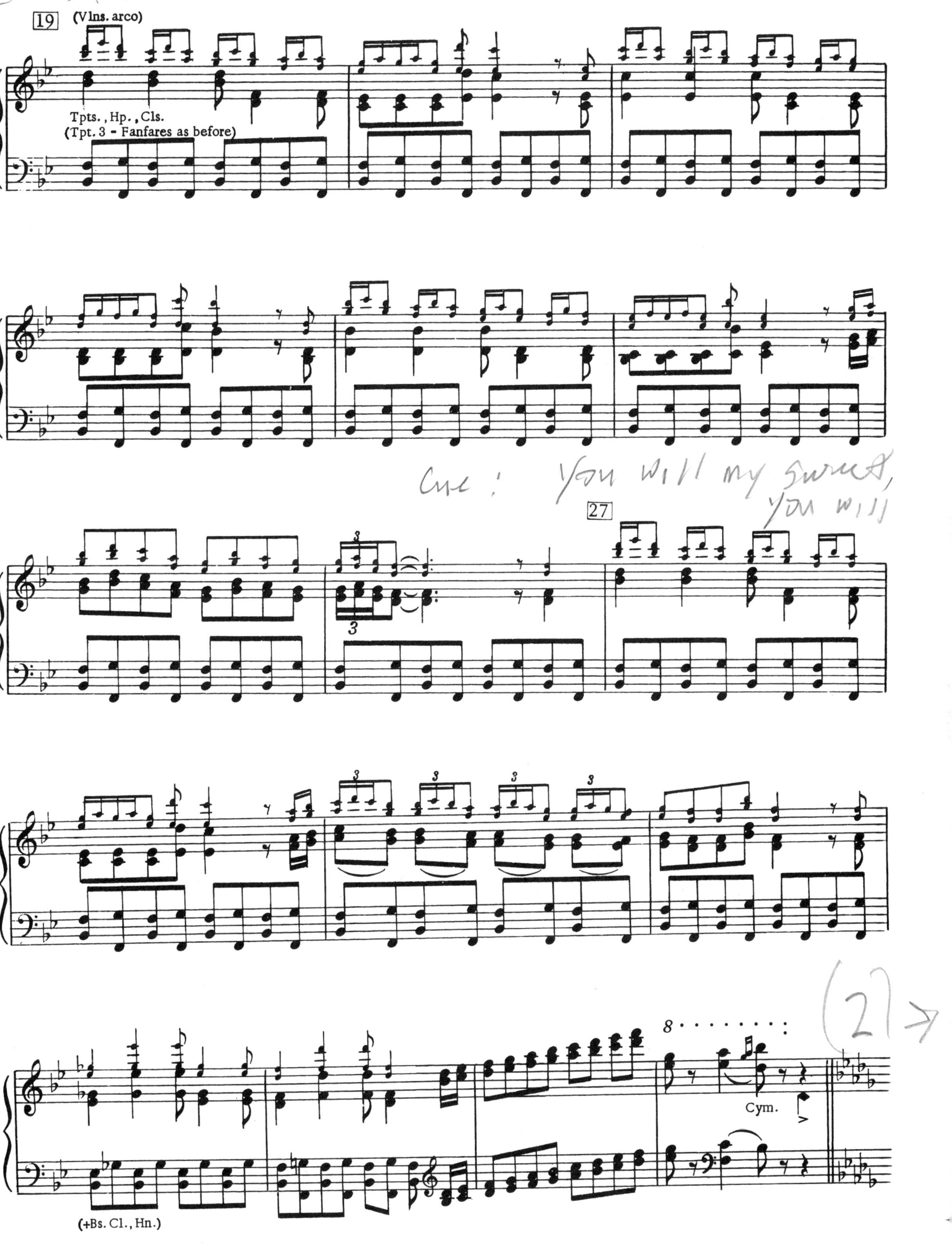
19
(Vlns. arco)
Tpts., Hp., Cls.
(Tpt. 3 - Fanfares as before)
Cue! You will my sweet, you will
27
8
Cym.
(+Bs. Cl., Hn.)
(2)

We Open In Venice

55
+ Mand., Hp.
+ Cls.
pens-ing fol-de - rol fri-vol - i - tee. Mere folk who give dis -
Br., Hn., Str.
ff
p
+ Mand.
Pno., Hp.
Str. pizz.
PETRUCHIO:
trac - tion are we, No The-a-tre Guild at - trac-tion are
+ 2 Cls.
simile
+ Hn.
+Hn.
63
ENSEMBLE:
W. W.
we. But just a cra-zy group that nev-er ceas-es to
+ 2 Cls.
Str. arco, div.
col 8va
+ Hn.
+ Hn.
Cello, Hn.
+ W. W., Br.
troop A - round the map of lit-tle I - tal - ee.
+ Hp.
Str.
Cl. 2
+ Hp.
+ Hp.
f
p
+ Br.
dim. e poco rall.
a tempo
Pno.
p
f
Cl. 1
Tpt.
Trb., B. Cl.

Refrain: 71 (Play 4 times)
ENSEMBLE:
1. We o-pen in Ven-ice, We next play Ve-ro-na, Then on to Cre-mo-na
SOLO:
(KATH.) Lots a laughs in Cre-mo-na.
(LUC.) Lots a bars in Cre-mo-na.
(BIA.) Lots a dough in Cre-mo-na.
(PETR.) Lots a quail in Cre-mo-na.
79
ENSEMBLE:
Our next jump is Par-ma. That stin-gy, din-gy, men-ace.
That beer-less, cheer-less, men-ace.
That do-pey, mo-pey, men-ace.
That heart-less, tart-less, men-ace.
Then Man-tu-a, Then Pa-du-a, Then we o-pen a-gain,
1.2.3. ending
Where? 2. We 3. We 4. We
Final ending
Where? In Ven-ice.
Mand.
Str., Cls.
Br., W. W.
Hn., low Str., B. Cl.
Str.
(W. W. sust.)
Br., W. W., Hp.
+ Hn.
+ B. Cl., Perc.
Br., W. W., Mand.
+ Hp.
sf
ff

Segue as one

No.5a

Dance

(End Padua Street Scene)

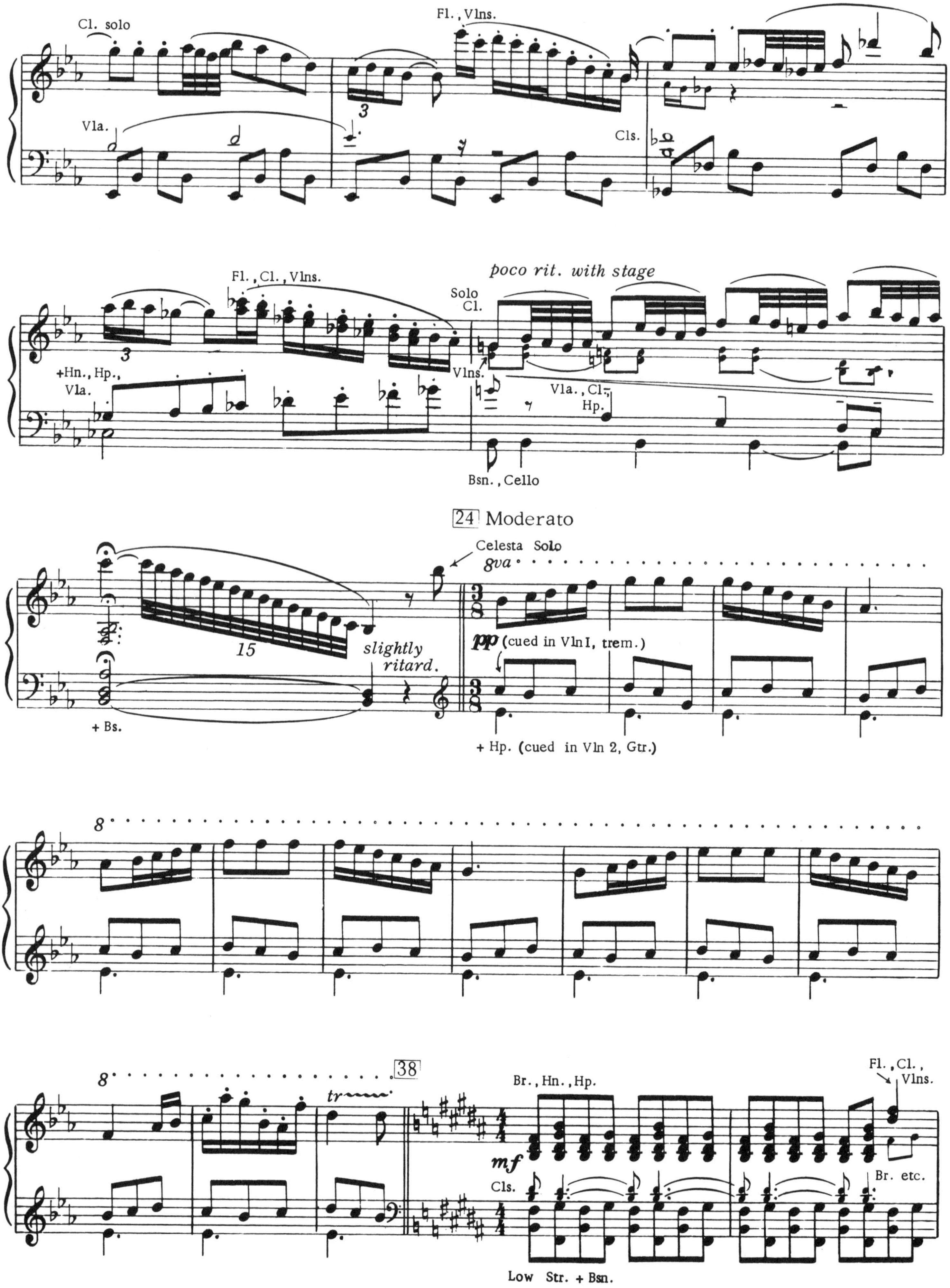
Cl. solo
Fl., Vlns.
Vla.
3
Cls.
Fl., Cl., Vlns.
poco rit. with stage
Solo
Cl.
3
+Hn., Hp.,
Vla.
Vlns.
Vla., Cl.
Hp.
Bsn., Cello
24 Moderato
Celesta Solo
8va
15
slightly
ritard.
pp (cued in Vln I, trem.)
+ Bs.
+ Hp. (cued in Vln 2, Gtr.)
8
8
38
tr
Br., Hn., Hp.
Fl., Cl.,
Vlns.
mf
Cls.
Br. etc.
Low Str. + Bsn.

(marcato)
Cls. cont.
+ Cls.
48
Xyl., Fl., Cl.
Vlns.
Cello, Hn.
Cello, Hn., Bsn.
+ Br.
+ Br., Vla.
+ Br.
Br.
3
(W. W., Trb. sust.)
Tpt., Vla.
Tpts.
Vlns.
W. W.
tr
Br.
Str. pizz.

No.6 Tom, Dick or Harry

Cue: BIANCA: Ah! me!

21
+ W. W.
purse has yet to know a sil - ver lin - ing. Still life - less is my
(pizz.)
Tpts ,Xyl.
Cello
W. W.
29
wife - less fam - i - ly tree. But if for love un - end - ing thou art
+ Tpts., Xyl.
Str. (pizz.)
HORTENSIO:
pin - ing, Mar - ry me, mar - ry me, mar - ry me. I
+ Tpts., Xyl.
+ Tpts., Xyl.
Str. arco
Hn.
37
+ Str.
W. W.
come to thee, a thor - ough - bred pa - tri - cian Still spray - ing my de -
Hp.
pp
Cello, Hn.

45
+ Str.
cay-ing fam-i-ly tree. To give a so-cial lift to thy po-
W. W. + Str.
Hp.
Cello, Hn.
W. W.
si - tion, Mar-ry me, mar-ry me, mar-ry me,
(+ Pno.)
(With exaggerated passion)
53
mar-ry me, mar-ry me! Mar-ry
GREMIO & LUCENTIO:
Mar-ry me! Mar-ry me!
Str.
(Slightly slower than Verse)
me! Mar-ry me!
GREMIO:
GREMIO & LUCENTIO:
Mar-ry me! Mar-ry me!
Br.
rall.

Refrain: 63
BIANCA:
I'm a maid who would mar-ry And will take with no qualm An-y
mp
Cl.
a tempo
Tom, Dick or Har-ry, An-y Har-ry, Dick or Tom. I'm a
71
maid mad to mar-ry And will take dou-ble quick An-y
GREMIO:
Tom, Dick or Har-ry, An-y Tom, Har-ry or Dick. I'm the
W. W.
Br.
mf
(pizz.)

79 Tempo di Fox-Trot (Slightly faster with a bounce)
+ Str.
BIANCA:
GREMIO:
LUCENTIO:
man thou should'st mar - ry. How - dy, Pop! How - dy Mom! I'm the
(W. W. sust.)
Br.
Hn., Cello
BIANCA:
HORTENSIO:
man thou should'st mar - ry. Art thou Har - ry, Dick or Tom? I'm the
Br.
pizz.
Cello
Vlns. arco
87
BIANCA:
HORTENSIO:
BIANCA:
man thou should'st mar - ry. How - dy, pal! How - dy, Chick! Art thou
Pno.
HORTENSIO:
Tom, Dick or Har - ry? Call me Tom, Har - ry or Dick.
(pizz.)

A Cappella
95
BIANCA:
I'm a maid who would mar - ry And would no long - er tar - ry; I'm a
SUITORS:
She's a maid who would mar - ry And would no long - er tar - ry; She's a
(Orch. tacet-cued in Str. + Hp.)
p
maid who would mar - ry; May my hopes not mis - car - ry! I'm a
maid who would mar - ry; May her hopes not mis - car - ry! She's a
103
maid mad to mar - ry, And will take dou - ble quick An - y
maid mad to mar - ry, And will take dou - ble quick An - y

107 Molto sostenuto (broad)
Tom, Dick or Har - ry, — an - y Tom, Har-ry or
Tom, Dick or Har - ry, — an - y Tom, Har-ry or —
Tutti Orch.
(+ Timp.)
113 Suddenly Hot Fox-Trot
Dick; A-dick-a - dick, A-dick-a - dick, A-dick-a - dick, A-dick-a-
Dick; A-dick-a - dick, A-dick-a - dick, A-dick-a - dick, A-dick-a-
Br. (8va bassa)
W. W.
Str. pizz.
(afterbeats)
Hn.
poco a poco cresc.
dick, A-dick-a - dick, A-dick-a - dick!
dick, A-dick-a - dick, A-dick-a - dick!
+ Br.
(all low inst.)
(Str. arco)
Tutti
Segue after applause

No.6a Encore-Tom, Dick or Harry

(Skat)
Dick or Har - ry, An - y Tom, Har-ry or Dick, Rah da-
Br., W. W.
Suitors exit
Dick or Har - ry,
Br., W. W.
Str.
Hn., Bsn.
Cello
21
da - dat-do - dat Doo - dah, Bo-da da rah, Bo-da-da
(Till off)
Dick, Dick, Dick, A-dick-a, Dick, Dick, Dick, A-dick-a, Dick, Dick
Cls.
tr
fp
Pno., Gtr.
+ Bsn.
rah do dah, Bo-da da rah, Bo-da da rah do dah, Bo-da da rah.
Dick, A-dick-a, Dick, Dick, Dick, A-dick-a, Dick.
f
Tutti
sfz

No.7 Rose Dance

Cue:LUCENTIO: ...washed with dew. Sweet Bianca.

19
Più mosso
f
L. H.
L. H.
27
rit.
L. H.
a tempo
Tpts., Cl.
Hn., Cello
rit.
35
Sempre animato
Hn., Cello
43

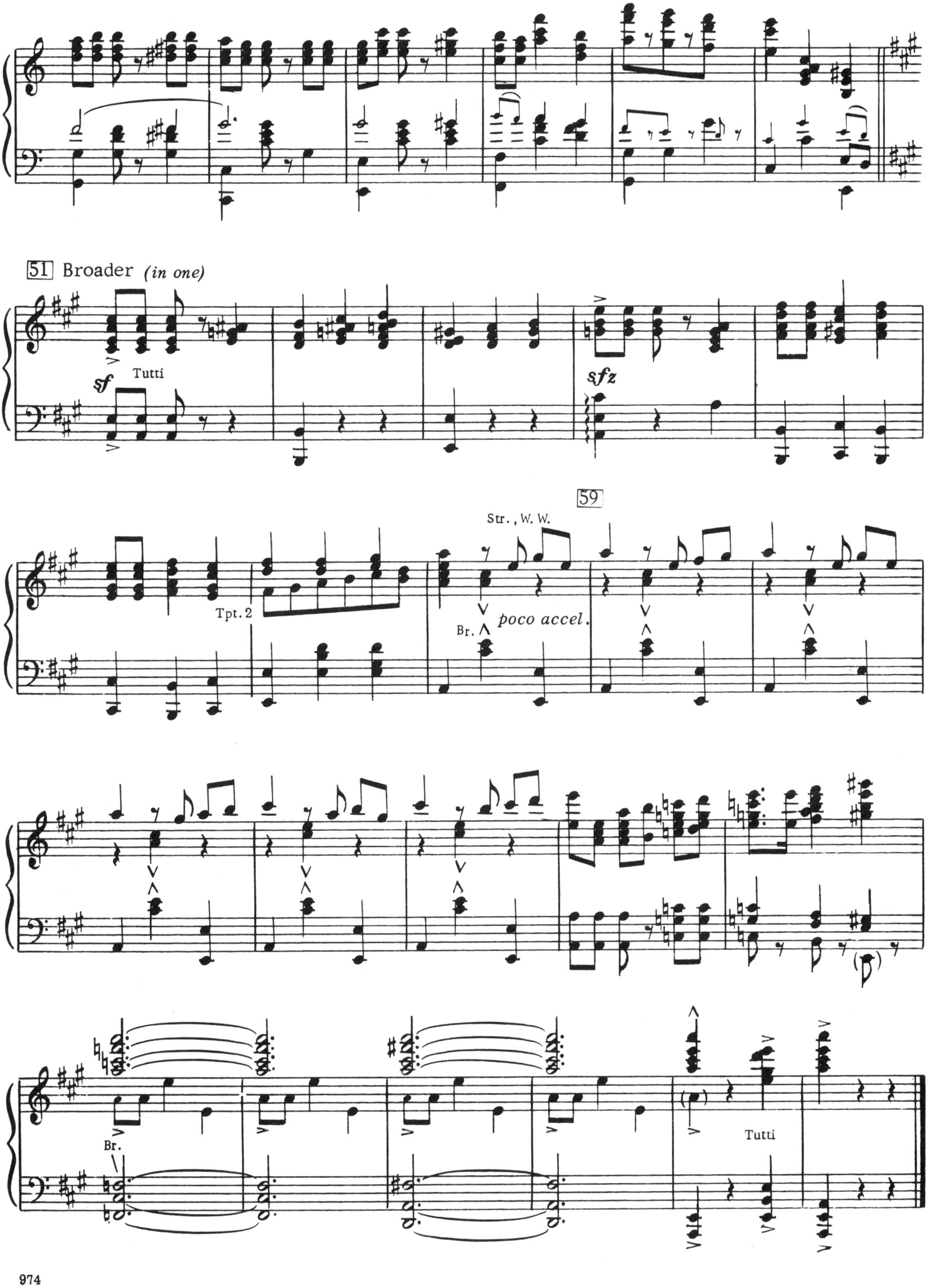
51 Broader (in one)
sf
Tutti
sfz
59
Str., W. W.
Tpt. 2
Br.
poco accel.
Br.
Tutti

2. Bob; Thus I'll visit her

No.8 I've Come To Wive It Wealthily In Padua

1. BOB. / Fall to them as you find your stomach serves you

Dialogue: PETRUCHIO: And the botany!

19
MALE CHORUS:
Str.
wealth - i-ly in Pa - du-a. He's come to wive it wealth - i-ly in
+ W. W. 8va
W. W.
(+ muted Br.)
mf Hn.
+ Timp.
PETRUCHIO:
Fl., E. H.
Pa - du-a. I heard you mut-ter "Zounds, a loath-some lad you are."
Vlns., Vlas.
+ Cl.
(Timp. tacet)
27
I shall not be dis-turbed a bit, If she be but a quart-er wit. If she
Bells, W. W.
Str.
Vla.
p
+ B. Cl.
+ Bsn.
can on-ly talk of clo'es While she pow-ders her dog-gone nose. (Hn.) I've
Bells, W. W.
Str., Cl.
E. H.
poco rit.
Hn.
+ B. Cl., Bsn.

MALE CHORUS:
come to wive it wealth - i - ly in Pa - du - a. He's
Str., W. W.
B. Cl., Bsn., Hn.
mf a tempo
+ Br.
39
W. W.
PETRUCHIO:
come to wive it wealth - i - ly in Pa - du - a. I
Hn., Str.
f
p
simile
heard you say "Gad - zooks, com-plete - ly mad you are." 'Twould-n't
Fl., Cl.
Hn.
Str.
p
All Str., Bsn., B. Cl.
47
give me the slight - est shock, If her knees, now and then, should knock, If her
W. W.
+ B. Cl.
+ Hp.
+ Hn.
+ Bsn.

eyes were a wee bit crossed, Were she wear-ing the hair she'd lost, Still the
55
dam-sel I'll make my dame, In the dark they are all the same. I've
W. W., Hp.
Str., W. W.
ten.
+ Hn.
a tempo
MALE CHORUS:
come to wive it wealth-i-ly in Pa-du-a. He's
Hn., Bsn., B. Cl.
+ Br.
63
PETRUCHIO:
come to wive it wealth-i-ly in Pa-du-a. I
W. W.
Hns., Str.
più f
Br., Cello, Bs.
sim.
p

heard you say "Good gad, but what a cad you are." Do I
Vlns.
+ E. H.
Str.
Vla., Hn., W. W.
p
(Br. out)
71
mind if she fret and fuss, If she fume like Ve-su - vi - us, If she
Xyl., Picc.
Cl., Xyl.
+ B. Cl.
+ Bsn.
Hn., E. H.
Hn., E. H.
(Bsn. cont.)
roar like a win - ter breeze On the rough A-dri-at - ic seas, If she
79
scream like a teeth - ing brat, If she scratch like a ti - ger cat, If she
etc.

Second time to ; 115

Steven - WAS ever gentleman thus grieved as I

No.9 I Hate Men

Cue: KATHERINE: ~~Lucentio, thou meacock wretch~~

1 vs

Cantabile
15 Gaily
I hate men. Of all the types I've ev - er met, with-
I hate men. If thou shouldst wed a bus'-ness man, Be
Str.
+ Hn.
Cls.
mp
Cello, Bsn.
pizz.
in our de - mo - cra - cy, I hate the most, the ath - lete with his
wa - ry, oh be wa - ry, He'll tell you he's de - tained in town on
Cls.
19
man - ner bold and brass - y. He may have hair up - on his chest, But
bus' - ness nec - es - sar - y. His bus' - ness is the bus' - ness which he
Str., W. W.
+ Cls.
+ Hp., Gtr.
1.
sis - ter, so has Las - sie, Oh, I hate men!
gives his sec - re - ta - ry, Oh, I hate men!
Str., W. W.
W. W.
Hp. Solo
Pno., Gtr.
f
+ Hn.
poco rit.
sff
Pno., Gtr., Hp.
Str.
p
8.
+ Timp.

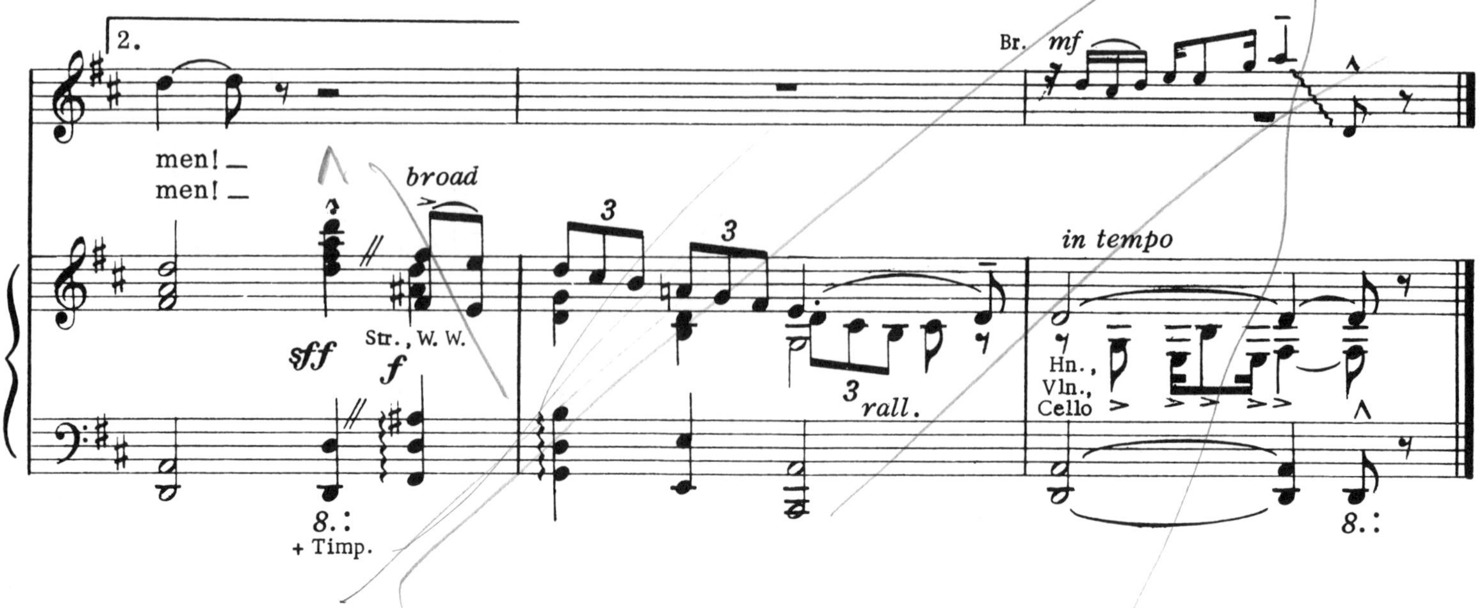

No.9a Encore-I Hate Men

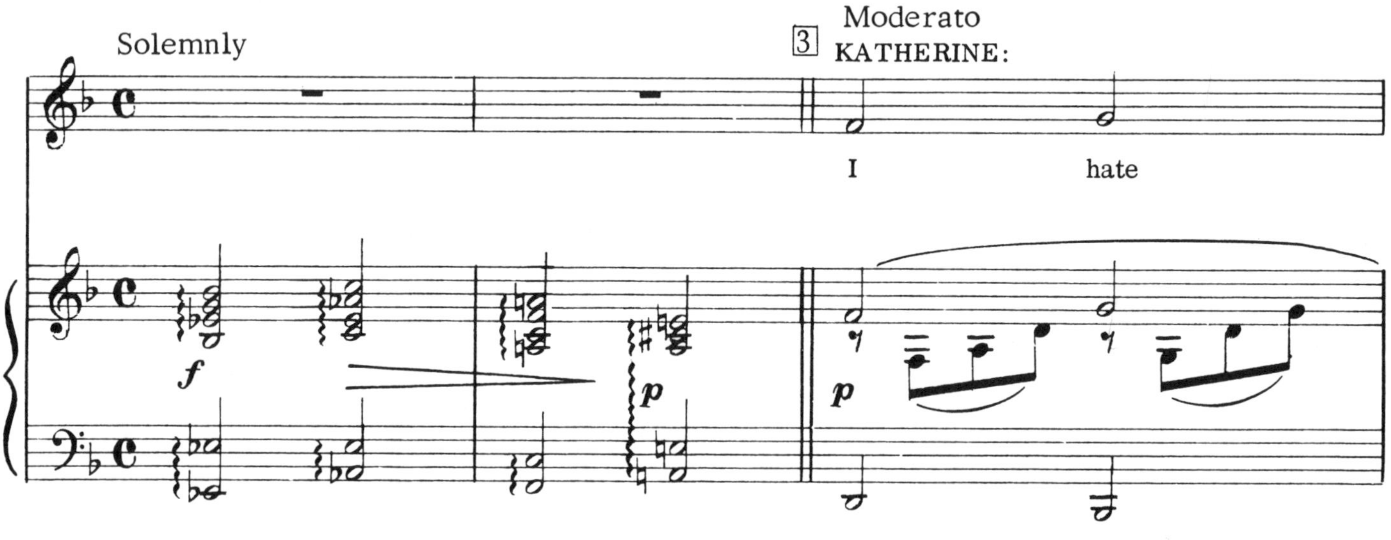

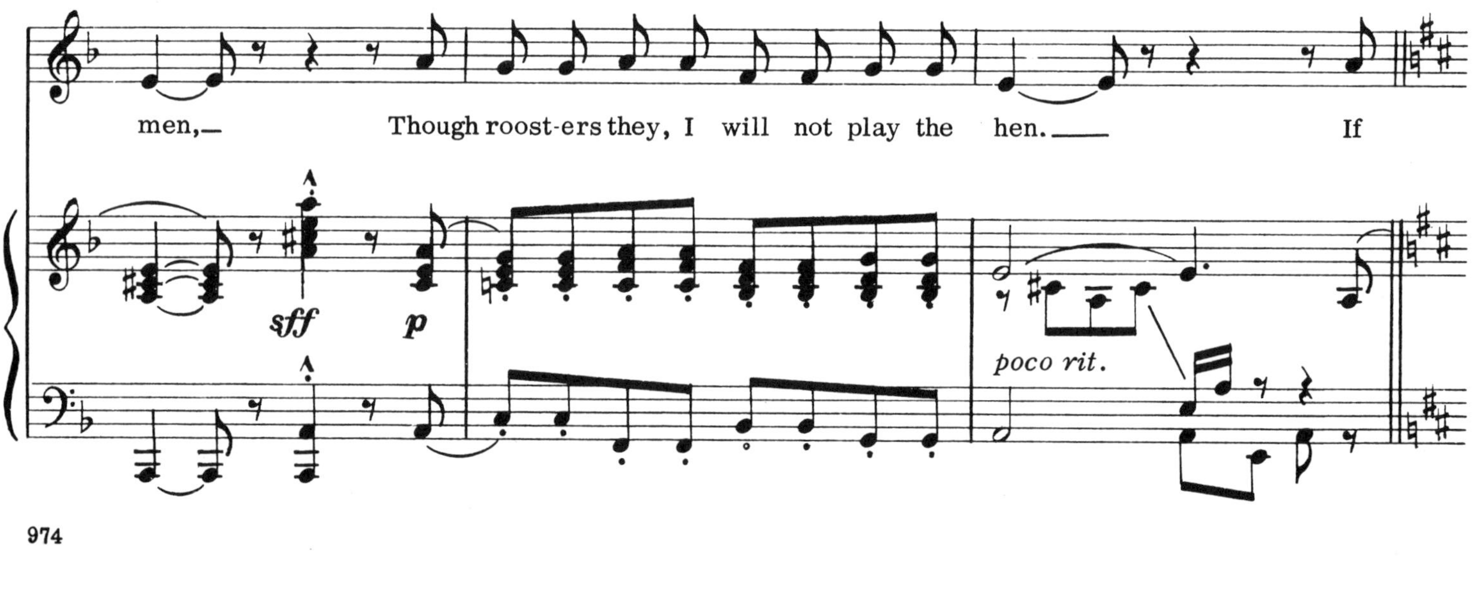

7
you es - pouse an old - er man; through girl - ish op - ti - mi - sm, He'll
etc.
al - ways stay at home at night and make no cri - ti - ci - sm. Though
you may call it "love" the doc - tors call it "rheu - ma - ti - sm," Oh
poco cresc. e rallentando
mf
15 Gaily
I hate men. From all I've read, a - lone in bed, From
broad with expression
Cls.
mp
Cello, Bsn.
pizz.

A to Zed, a - bout 'em, Since love is blind, then from the mind, All
Cls.
wom - an - kind should rout 'em. But la - dies, you must an - swer too, What
Str., W. W.
+ Cls.
+Hp., Gtr.
would we do with - out 'em? Still I hate
Str., W. W.
f + Hn.
poco rit.
men!
Br. mf
sff
broad
rall.
in tempo

No.10 Were Thine That Special Face

Cue: PETRUCHIO: Ay-there's the rub.

ten - der, Were thine the kiss di - vine. Were
p dolce
(Tpts. tacet)
+ Tpts.
27
thine the love for me, The love which fills my
Str., W. W. Hp.
Hn., Cello
Vln., Vla.
35
dream - ing, When all these charms are thine,
+ Hn.
Str., W. W
cresc.
Hn.
Tpts.
rit.
Then you'll be mine, all mine.
f
a tempo
Str., Cls., E. H.
Str., W. W.
Hn.

43
Quasi recitativo and tenderly
I wrote a po - em in class - ic style
E. H. Solo
Cl.
p dolce
B. Cl.
Hp. (cued in Str. & Pno.)
I wrote it with my tongue in my cheek And my lips in a smile.
+Hn.
51
But of late my po - em Has a mean-ing so new, For, to
Solo Vln. 8va
Fl. 8 bassa
+E. H.
pp
Str.
(Fl., B. Cl. sust.)
(no Bs.)
Hp.
mp
Str., Cls.
poco sostenuto
my sur - prise, It sud - den - ly ap - plies to my dar - ling, To

Moderato a la beguine
Fl.
60
(+ Vlns. div., Vla. sust.)
you. Were thine that
Pno., Hp., Gtr.
Pno., Hp.
mf B. Cl., E. H.
+ Gtr.
p
(pizz.)
spec - ial face, The
Cls.
face which fills my dream - ing. Were
Tpts. muted
Cls.
68
(Vlns. div., Vla. sust.)
thine the rhy - thm'd grace, Were
Cls.

+ Cello
thine the form so lithe and slen - der, Were
Str., Cls. sust.
Cls.
76
thine the arms so warm, so ten - der, Were
(+ E. H.)
Vlns.
Cls.
+ Vlns.
thine the kiss di - vine. Were
Tpts.
Vla., Cello
Str., W. W. sust.
84
Vlns. div., (Vla. sust.)
thine the love for me, The
Pno., Hp., Gtr.
Cls.

Tpts.
love which fills my dream - ing When
Cls.
92
all these charms are thine, Then you'll be mine,
+ Br.
+ Br.
(Str. sust.)
Tutti cresc.
sf
a tempo
+ Timp.
E.H., B.Cl.
all mine.
Hn., Trb., low Str. melody

104
Dance
Beguine tempo
Vlns. pizz.
Pno., Hp., Gtr.
3
mf (Bring out thumb)
Fl., E.H., Cl.
Vlns. arco, Cls.
Tpts.
Fl., E.H., Cl.
112
Vlns. pizz.
Fl., E.H., Cl.
Vlns.

118 - 166

Vlns. arco., Cls.
Tpts.
(Tpts. cont.)
pizz.
120
Fl., E.H., Cl.
Cls.
+ Tpts.
Pizz. Vlns.
W. W.
W. W.
Hp., Pno., Gtr.
Str., Tpts. div.
128
Br.
Hn.,
Vla., Cello

Vlns. pizz.
Fl., E. H., Cl.
Vlns. arco, Cls.
Fl., E. H., Cl.
Vlns. pizz.
Voce
136
arco
Trb., Hn., low Str.
143
W. W.
Pno., Hp., Gtr.
All Str., Br., Hn.
R. H.
+ Pno., Hp., Gtr.

B. Cl.
151
simile
+ Hn. ,Str.
p
(Rhythm continues)
W. W. 8va
+ Hn. ,Str.
W. W. 8va

159
Vlns., Vla.
f
(Rhythm)
etc.
(legato)
167
Br.
W. W.
Br.
Hp.
etc.
Hn., Str.
mf
simile

W. W.
Br.
175
PETRUCHIO:
When all those
p
W. W., (Trb. sust.)
179
charms are thine,
(Br.)
Then you'll be mine
W. W., Str. div.
all
mine.
etc.
Str.
cresc.

No.11 Change of Scene

Cue: PETRUCHIO: All right, Miss Vanessi, you asked for this, and you're going to get it.

No.11a Change of Scene

(Scene 6-7)

Cut

Cue: FRED: That's all I need---a blind stage manager.

Cut Cut - ~~True Love with flaws~~ From this ~~moment~~ on

No.12 I Sing of Love

Cue: FRED: This is an outrage.

Allegro con gioia

Vamp
CHORUS: + Fl., Ob.
We
Hn., Trb., Cello
mf
Cls., Hp., Pno.
R. H.
Bs.
+ Cello,
Bsn.
27
sing of love, we
Str.
p
(W. W. sust.)
Vla.
Cello
sing on - ly of love Ye
Hn.
35
Gods a - bove, May we

+ Fl., Ob.
nev - er sing of an - y - thing but love. For
W. W. 8va
pp
Hn., Cello
43
W. W.
(+ Hp., Pno.)
love is the joy of ev - 'ry girl and boy, As
Vlns. 15va
+ Vla.
Bsn., Vla., Cello
Br.
love, lat - er on, keeps 'em go - ing 'til they're gone. Yes,
Cls. Soli
+ Hn.
51
+ Xyl., Hp.
love is the theme of all peo - ple who dream, So
+ Ob., Str.
Str.
f
(Bsn., Cello sust.)

love, let's con - fess, is ev - 'ry - bod - y's bus - i -
poco rall.
W. W.
+Bsn., Trb., Cello
61
ness. Oh, ye Gods a - bove,
Vlns., Pno., Hp.
a tempo
Str.
p (W. W. sust.)
May we nev - er sing of an - y - thing but love, sweet
Str., W. W.
+ Tpt. 2
+ Tpt. 3
cresc.
Hn.
Tutti
(Str. trem.)
(+ Timp.)
Patter: (marciale)
1st MAN:
71
love. I won't sing a song a - bout
Str., W. W.
Tutti
Str., W. W.
sf
mf
p
+ Hn.

1st GIRL:
2nd MAN:
bat - tle. I won't sing of ba - bies who prat - tle. I get no glee from
+ Br.
mf
p
3rd MAN:
2nd GIRL:
songs a - bout the sea, or cow - boy songs a - bout cat - tle. I
cresc.
Str.
79
+ Fl., Bsn.
CHORUS:
won't waste a note of my pat - ters On so - cial - ly sig - ni - fi - cant mat - ters. We
(+ W. W.)
Br.
sing of one thing And we a - dore it, Thank heav - en for it! We
+ W. W.
(+ Hp., arp.)
Tutti
fz

87
sing of love, We
Str.
W. W.
Rhythm
mp
+ Br.
Hn.
Br.
sing only of love. Ye
+ Br.
+ Br.
95
Gods above, May we
W. W.
etc.
W. W.
Rhythm
+ Br.
Hn.
Br.
Str.
BIANCA:
never sing of anything but love. For
Br. div.
W. W.
Hn., Cello

103
love is the joy of ev - 'ry girl and boy. As
Hn., Bsn.
etc.
Br.
Br.
Str. pizz.
LUCENTIO:
Br.
love, lat - er on, keeps 'em go - ing till they're gone. Yes,
Str. arco div.
Bsn., Hn.
111
W. W.
love is the theme of all peo - ple who dream. So,
Bsn., Hn.
Bs.
ALL:
love, let's con - fess, is ev - 'ry - bod - y's bus - i -
poco rall.
Hn.
Trb., Bsn., Cello

121
ness. Oh, Ye Gods a - bove May we nev - er sing of an - y - thing but love, sweet love.
+ Str. unis.
Tpts.
a tempo
fz
mp
Hn.
+ Br.
Br.
Str. + 8va
W. W.
+ Trb.
129
ten.
Str., W. W. 8va
W. W. 8va
ff
ff + Br. 8va
+ Hn., Trb.
+ Timp.
Tutti
sfz
Hp.
p
Segue as one

No.12a Dance-Tarantella

29
W. W.
Hn., Tpt. 1
sfz
Str.
mp
Str.
simile
W. W.
p
f
W. W.
41
Vlns., W. W. 8va
f
+ Br.
ff
Str., W. W.
Pno.
+ Br.
Str.
Tpts.
Tutti

49
Str., W. W.
Br.
W. W., Xyl.
57
+ Br. (p)
+ Pno., Str.
65
+ Hn.
Br. 8 bassa
+ Trb.
Str., W. W.

73
W. W., Str.
Br.,
Hn.,
Hp.
Str.
Str.
Str.
W. W. 8va
f
Br.
Trb., Cello
ff
W. W.
fp
+ Hn.
fp
83
Str.
Str., Hn.
W. W.
mp
(Hn. tacet)
simile
Hp., Pno.
(W. W.)
95

Str.
103
W. W.
Muted Br., Str.
f
Hp.
(Pno. tacet)
W. W.
+ Br. div.
111
Str., W. W.
+ Hn.
+ Pno.
+ Br.
+ W. W.
+ Br.
f
119
(+ Hp. gliss.)
ff
(+ Hp. gliss.)

127
(+ Hp. gliss.)
+ Br. open
(+ Hp. gliss.)
8
137
Vlns., W. W.
Br.
mf
Str., Pno.
145
8va
3
f
3
Str.
p
f

W. W., Pno.
Str.
mf
Tutti
f
157
(Br. out)
Tpts.
Trb.
Tutti unis.
169
Tpt. 1
W. W.
f
Hn.
Str.
p
f
8.:

W. W.
177
Vlns. ,W. W. 8va
f
+ Br.
ff
Str., W. W.,
Pno.
+ Br.
Str.
Tpts.
185
Coda
Tutti
ff
193
fp
W. W. tr

Bob— (Look at him)

No.13 He dare to Finale Act I

Cue: PETRUCHIO: Stop my way in Padua!

10
(♩. = ♩)
ff
(+ Hp., Xyl.)
No! Go! Nay!
mf
kiss me, Kate, Thou love-ly loon, Ere we start On our
kiss him, Kate, Thou love-ly loon, Ere you start On your
(W. W. col Chorus)
mf
Str., Pno., Gtr.
Hp.
A-way! Fred!
hon-ey-moon, Oh, kiss me, Kate Dar-ling, dev-il di-vine.
hon-ey-moon, Oh, kiss him, Kate Dar-ling, dev-il di-vine.
+Br.

Allegro
17
mf
Kind - ly drop dead!
Now I shall nev - er be
For now thou shall ev - er be
Allegro
17
p
sf
sf
Now I shall nev - er be
thine
Not
mf cresc.
Now thou shall ev - er be
GIRLS-PRINCIPALS and SINGERS:
Yes, mine
mf cresc.
Now thou shall ev - er be
Now thou shall nev - er be
W. W.
Pno., Hp.
+ Br., W. W.
cresc.
sf
Str., Gtr.
thine
You
swine
You
swine
Yes, mine
Yes, mine
Yes, mine, So
MEN & GIRLS:
She called him a swine
+ Br. - - -
ff
Hn.

25
ff
I'll crack your pate, I'll
mp
kiss me, Kate, Oh, please don't pout,
25
Str., W. W., Pno.
+ Picc.
3
p sub.
mf sub.
knock you out. I'll black your eyes,
mf
My price - less prize! Oh,
(+ Picc.)
Your rump I'll kick, Bound-er!
Br.
kiss me quick! Oh, kiss me!
Oh, kiss him! He's
mp sub.
f
(+Hp. arp.)
Timp.
Str.

Ob., Cl.
ff
Oh, kiss me!
ff
not her dish, he's not her dish, Oh, kiss him!
+ W. W., Hn.
Bsn.
+ Bsn.
mf
+ Hp. arp.
Timp.
Gtr., Str. trem.
Ob., Cl.
41
Br.
Flound-er!
Picc.
ff
Oh, kiss me!
mp sub.
ff
A type of fish she would not wish, Oh, kiss him!
Str., Gtr., Pno.
+W. W., Hn.
41
p sub.
Str.
mf
+ Hp. arp.
Gtr., Str. trem.
ff
Ob., Cl.
Br.
Das-tard!
ff
Oh, kiss me!
mp
ff
What's that we heard? What's that we heard? Oh, kiss him!
+ W. W., Hn.
pp sub.
p sub.
Str.
+ Bsn.
mf
+ Hp. arp.
Timp.
(Str., Gtr. trem.)

Ob., Cl.
Bas - tard!
Picc.
Gasp
Oh,
ff GIRLS:
Oh! Kat - ie! that's a naught - y word, Oh,
+W. W., Hn.
Stop
Gasp
Str.
p sub.
49
kiss me! Kiss me! Kiss me!
cresc.
ALL:
Kiss him, Kiss him, Kiss him, Kiss him,
kiss him, Kiss him, Kiss him, Kiss him,
+ Br.
mp
8va
Quasi Cadenza
Angrily
KATE:
Nev-er, nev-er, nev - er, nev - er, nev - er,
più f
Picc.
(echo)
sf

KATE:
Slowly
nev - er, nev-er, nev - er, nev-er, nev-er, nev-er, nev-er, nev-er, nev-er, nev-er, nev-er, nev - er!
GIRLS:
pp
Oh,
TENORS:
pp
Oh,
PETRUCHIO and BASSES:
pp
Oh,
Stop! Joke--- (bird and shot)
pp
Hp.
61 Lively
GIRLS: cresc. poco a poco
Kiss him, Kate, Kiss him, Kiss him, Kate, Kiss him,
TENORS:
Kiss him, Kate, Kiss him, Kiss him, Kate, Kiss him,
PET. & BASSES:
Kiss me, Kate, Kiss me, Kiss me, Kate, Kiss me,
61
Saxs.
Str. (+ Picc. tr on F)
mp
Hn., Trb.
fp
fp
Cello
cresc. poco a poco
+ Timp.

69 (♩ = 𝅗𝅥) (in 1)
Kiss him, Kate, Kiss him, Kiss him, Kate, Kiss him, Kiss him, Kate,
Kiss him, Kate, Kiss him, Kiss him, Kate, Kiss him, Kiss him, Kate,
Kiss me, Kate, Kiss me, Kiss me, Kate, Kiss me, Kiss me, Kate,
+ Tpts.
fp
Hp.
(+ Vln., Vla., Picc. tr on F)
cresc. poco
Kiss him, Kate, Kiss him, Kate, Kiss him, Kate, Kiss him, Kate, Kiss him, Kate,
Kiss him, Kate, Kiss him, Kate, Kiss him, Kate, Kiss him, Kate, Kiss him, Kate,
Kiss me, Kate, Kiss me, Kate, Kiss me, Kate, Kiss me, Kate, Kiss me, Kate,
a poco
fz

KATE:
GANGSTER:
(spoken) Aw-kiss him.
(scream)
(scream)
Kiss him, Kate,_ Kiss him, Kate,_ Kiss him,
Kiss him, Kate,_ Kiss him, Kate,_ Kiss him,
Kiss me, Kate,_ Kiss me, Kate,_ Kiss me,
fz
fz
Tutti
Timp.
ff
81 Presto (+ Picc., Str., Altos tr.)
fff
Kate.
fff
Kate.
fff
Kate.
81 Presto
fff Tutti
+ Timp.
etc.

End of Act 1

No.14 Entr'acte

19 Tempo di Valse Viennese
Vlns., Vla., Fl., Cl.
Br., Saxs., Gtr.
mp
+ Cello
27 Very Viennese
mf
Tpts., Hn., rhythm
43
W. W., Str. (+8va)
+ W. W., Trb.
Tpts., Hn., Pno., Gtr.
Trb., Bar. Sax.
51

Fl., Cl.
Str., Br.
59
p +Hn.
mf (Saxs. sust.)
+ Trb.
67
75 Moderato-in 4
Br., Str.
Cl. Solo 8va
mf
+ Saxs.
(Cl. loco) Str.
Br. muted
R.H.
Hn. Solo
81
dolce
Vlns., Vla.
Saxs.
Cello
Br., Hp.

Vlns., Vla.
Br., Hp.
Alto 1
89
(Vlns. cont.)
(+ Hp. arp. ---)
Vlns.
Saxs.
+ Vln.
Br.
Br. Soli
Cello
97
Vlns., Vla.
Saxs., Hp.
Cello, Tenor
R. H.
etc.
(Violin Solo)

105 Tempo ad lib.
Vln. Solo (8va)
Hn., Vln., Vla.
(Piano Solo)
Br. open
Cello, W. W.
+ Saxs. (p)
f
(Bs. tacet)
111 Beguine
Str. 8va
mf
+ Pno., Hp., Gtr.
Br.
Saxs.
Saxs. Soli
Trb.
119
Br.
127
Br. Soli
Br. div.

Segue after Conductor's bow

Attaca

No.15

Act II
Too Darn Hot

25
__ with my ba-by to-night, __ And play the pup __
__ for my ba-by to-night, __ And blow my top __
__ with my ba-by to-night, __ Break ev-'ry rule __
(Tpt., Trb. opt.)
__ with my ba-by to-night. __ I'd like to sup __ with my
__ with my ba-by to-night. __ I'd like to stop __ for my
__ with my ba-by to-night. __ P. & BOYS: I'd like to fool __ with my
Saxs., Str. arco
mp
Rhythm
ba-by to-night, __ And play the pup __ with my ba-by to-night, __ But
ba-by to-night, __ And blow my top __ with my ba-by to-night, __ But I'd
ba-by to-night, __ Break ev-'ry rule __ with my ba-by to-night, __ But
1. 2.
I ain't up __ to my ba-by to-night __ 'Cause it's too darn hot. BOYS: It's
be a flop __ with my ba-by to-night __ 'Cause it's too darn hot. BOYS: It's
pil-low, you'll __ be my ba-by to-night __ 'Cause it's too darn
Str., Bar. Sax.
+Saxs.
p

3.
38
*
1st Refrain
hot. PAUL & BOYS: Ac - cord - ing to the Kin - sey re - port Ev - 'ry
Br., Vlns. 8va
Saxs., Cello, Vla.
av - er - age man you know Much pre - fers to play his fav -
Saxs.
our - ite sport When the tem - pe - ra - ture is low, But
when the ther - mo - me - ter goes 'way up And the
Tutti
8

* Orch. parts retain "G" signature throughout vocal.

50
weath-er is sizz-ling hot
PAUL: Mis-ter A-dam For his
(Br. tacet)
Vlns.
mf
Saxs., Str.
p
Ten. Sax.
Rhythm
mad-am Is not.
P. & BOYS: 'Cause it's too, too, Too darn
Str.
Saxs.
Hn.
Br.
Orch. unis.
mp
hot, It's too darn hot, It's
58
(Vln. cues)
too. darn hot
PAUL: It's
Br., Saxs.
f
+ Trb., Hn., Bar.

62
Play 3 times
too darn hot, It's too darn hot, I'd
PAUL: I'd
PAUL: I'd
Str. unis.
Saxs.
Rhythm
Alto, Bar.
(+ Tpt. opt.)
like to call on my ba-by to-night, And
like to meet with my ba-by to-night, Get
like to coo to my ba-by to-night, And
+ pizz. Str.
70
(+ Tpt., Trb.)
give my all to my ba-by to-night, P. & BOYS: I'd
off my feet with my ba-by to-night, I'd
pitch the woo with my ba-by to-night, I'd
like to call on my ba-by to-night, And give my all to my
like to meet with my ba-by to-night, Get off my feet with my
like to coo to my ba-by to-night, And pitch the woo with my
Saxs., Str. arco

(Tpt. opt.)
79
ba - by to - night, PAUL: But I can't play ball_ with my ba - by to - night_'Cause it's
ba - by to - night,_ But no re - peat_ with my ba - by to - night_'Cause it's
ba - by to - night,_ But, broth - er, you_ bite my ba - by to - night_'Cause it's
+ Saxs.
1.2.
3.
too darn hot. P. & BOYS: It's hot. P. & BOYS: Ac -
too darn hot. BOYS: It's
too darn
Vlns. 8va
Br.
83
2nd Refrain:
cord-ing to the Kin - sey re-port Ev-'ry a-ver-age man you know_ Much pre-
Saxs.
Saxs., Vla., Cello
fers to play his fav - our-ite sport When the tem-per-a-ture is low. But
Tutti

when the ther-mo-me-ter goes 'way up And the weath-er is sizz - lin'
95 parlando
hot, Mis-ter Gob For his squab, A mar - ine For his
Vlns.
Saxs., Str.
pp
+Ten. Sax.
Vln.
queen, A G. I. For his cut-ie pie_ Is not. 'Cause it's too, too,
Orch. unis.
103
Str.
Too darn hot. It's too darn hot It's too,__ too,_
Saxs.
Hn.
Br.
mf
Str.
p
+Pno.

too, too, darn hot.
+Br. open
pp (Gtr., Pno.)
ff
Tutti
DANCE
1 Bright Fox-trot
Saxs., Pno.
mf
Br.
+Trb., 2 Saxs.
Br. (in hat)
+ Rhythm
+ 2 Saxs.
13 Cls. (Alto 8 bassa)
Tpt. (open)
Low Saxs., Rhythm
Br. open
+Bar.

etc.
Tacet for break
2
2
+ Br.
+ Bar.
25
(Rhythm)
Hn., Str.
2 Saxs.
mf
Ten., Bar.
Vlns., Vla.
Br., Saxs.
(Br., Gtr.)
Ten., Bar.
etc.
33
Cls., Saxs.
Hot!
Dr. Soli
Hot!
Too hot!
Too hot!
Too darn hot!
Too darn hot!
Br., W. W.
+ Trb., Bar.
(Dr. cont.)
41
Tpt. Solo (muted)
div.
(Saxs. sust.)

Br.open
49
Str.
Saxs.
Br.
57
Saxs.
div.
(simile)
Str.

etc.
69
Hp., Str. pizz. (octaves)
Br. 8va
mf
3 Cls.
cresc.
Hp., Str. pizz. (octaves)
Br. 8va
Tpt. 1 Solo
Pno.
77
(ad lib.)
Vlns., Vla.
Hp.
Ten. Sax.
Brass, Rhythm
W. W., Vlns.

85
Vla., Cello (sust.)
sim.
Br.
Br.
W. W.
Br.
Hn., Str.
Cymb.
97
Orch. unis.
Cymb. Solo
Hn.
Br.
Str. pizz.
etc.
W. W.
Hn., W. W.

+ Br.
3
3
+ Str. arco
Cl. Solo
109
Br.
mp
Gtr., Pno. (chords)
Cls. (Saxs. 8 bassa)
Solo Cl.
Cls. (Saxs. 8 bassa)
Solo Cl.
117
(+ Str. sust.)
Saxs.
etc.
Br.

125
Vlns.
Tpts., Hns.
fp
Trb.
W. W. Saxs.
(+ Vlns.)
f
3
+ Trb.
f
p
Trb.
W. W. Saxs.
Br.
Cl.
Hn., Pno.

Tpt. 2
Br., Cl.
Saxs., Hn.
Cello, Bs., Pno.
Presto
145
Cl., Br., Hn. div.
(+ Vlns., Vla.)
(simile)
Vlns., Vla.
153
Tutti
Tutti unis.
Segue

Too Darn Hot-Bows

Cut

Cue: RALPH: On stage everybody!

L'istesso tempo

No.15a

Change of Scene

Cue: FRED: Thank you.

25
+ Tpts.
Hn., Cello
Cymb.
+ Trb., Sax.
Open Br., Str.
33
(Tpts. out)
Saxs., Vla., Cello
mf
(+ Hn.)
Ten., Cello
Bs.
41
cresc. più espr.
Hn., Ten. Sax.
etc.
poco marc.

 * 4 bar 1st ending inserted in orch. parts.

+ B. D., Hp.

Bob! sweet Kate - what life there is in store for me

No. 16 Where Is The Life That Late I Led?

Cue: PETRUCHIO: She has performed, while I did act the dolt.

19
Br., Xyl.
(+E. H.)
show that's typ - i - cal - ly Shu - bert - y, I have
al - ways had a mult - i - tude of girls. But
+ W. W.
Vla.
+ Hn.
27
much broader-ad lib.
now that a mar - ried man, at last, am I, How a-
Str., Hp., Pno.
W. W., Str. 8va
mp
ware of my dear, de - part - ed past am I. Where is the
Tempo I
W. W. sust., Str. trem.
pp
fp
Tutti
sff
+Cym.

35
Refrain:
life that late I led? Where is it
Str.
mf
Cello
+ Bsn.
Br. div.
now? To-tal-ly dead. Where is the
Hn.
43
fun I used to find? Where has it
Str.
Cello
+ Vla., Hn., E.H.
W. W. div.
gone? Gone with the wind. A
Br., W. W.
W. W.
Bsn.
+ Cello

51
mar - ried life may all be well But
f Vla., Cello
+Br.
subito p
Vln.
rais-ing an heir Could nev-er com-pare With rais-ing a bit of
Str.
59
hell. So I re - peat what first I said, Where is the
mf
Hn., E. H.
Hn.
life that late I, In dear Mi - la - no, where are you,
66
Bells
f
Vlns.
+Mand.
Str.
+ Timp.

Mo - mo, Still sell - ing those pic - tures of the scrip - tures in the
Duo - mo? And Ca - ro - li - na, Where are you Li - na, Still ped - dling your
Cl.
Str. pizz.
Cls.
E. H., Vla., Cello
+ Mand.
Cls.
Bsn.
piz - za in the streets o' Ta - or - mi - na? And in Fi - ren - ze, where are you,
74
Bells
+ Hp.
Str. arco
pizz.
p
A - lice, Still there in your pret - ty, it - ty - bit - ty Pit - ti pal - ace? And sweet Luc-
Ob., Cls.
Cello, Hp.
B. Cl. rit.

* Pronounced "Caroleena" ** "Leena" *** "peetsa"

Mand.
etc.
re - tia, so young and gay - ee? What scan - da - lous
Str. pizz.
Vlns., Vla. arco
do - in's in the ru - ins of Pom - pe - ii! Where is the
sf
Tutti
rit.
a tempo
82
life that late I led? (Tpts. muted) Where is it
Str., Mand.
+ Fls.
+ Hp.
p
Cello
Bs. pizz.
now? To - tal - ly dead. Where is the
Tpts.
W. W.
+ Tpts.

90
fun I used to find? Where has it
Str., Mand.
+Hp.
W. W.
Tpts.
Cello
+ Vla.
Bs. pizz.
gone? Gone with the wind. The
Tpts.
pp
+ Br.
98
mar - riage game is quite al - right. Yes,
Vlns.
dur - ing the day it's eas - y to play, But oh, what a bore at night. So I re -
+ Mand.
p

peat what first I said: Where is the life
Str., Mand.
+ Hp.
Fls.
+ W. W.
Cello
Vla.
Hn.
Bs. pizz.
113
that late I Where is Re - bec - ca, my Beck-i - weck - io? Could still she be
Vlns., Mand.
W. W., Bells
Trb., Cello
Vla., Cello, Hp.
+ Trb.
+ Timp.
cruis - ing that a-mus - ing Pon - te Vecch-io? Where is Fe - do - ra, The wild vi-
+ Fls.
Cello, Hp.
+ Br.
Vla.
B. Cl.
(+ Mand.)
ra - go? It's luck - y I missed her gang-ster sis - ter from Chi - ca - go. Where is Ve -
Vlns., Mand + 8va
(+ Mand.)
+ Hp.
Hp.
B. Cl.

* Pronounced "Leeza"

137
To - tal - ly dead.
Where is the fun I
+ Tpts. (Str. trem.)
W. W. 8va
+ E. H., Mand.
+ Hn., Trb. open
Hp. gliss.
Str.
Cello, Hn.
used to find?
Where has it gone?
Tpts.
145
Gone with the wind.
I've oft' been told of
Str., Pno.
W. W.
E. H.
(+ Hp.)
ff
fz p
p + E. H.
ad lib.
nup - tial bliss,
But what do you do, at quar-ter to two, With
Str., Pno.

153
a tempo
W. W.
on - ly a shrew to kiss? So I re - peat what first I said:
Str., W. W.
Muted Br., Vlns 8va
+ Hn., Vla.
Cello
+ Hn.
etc.
ad lib.
Where is the life that late I
W. W.
+ E. H.
Str., W. W.
(+ Timp., pp)
Timp.
161 Prestissimo
(Vlns. tr.)
Hp.
led?
Br. open, W. W. 8va
+ Hp.
cresc.
tr
+ Timp.
Segue

No. 16a Change Of Scene

ad lib.
Str., Pno.
25
Str., W. W.
Muted Br., Vla. 8va
+ Hn., Vla.
Cello
+Hn.
Str., W. W.
(+ Timp., pp)
W. W.
+ E. H.
Timp.
33
Br. open, W. W. 8va
+ Hp.
cresc.
+ Timp.

No.17 Always True To You In My Fashion

Cue: LOIS: ... and wants to get along--with her fellow man!

18
Medium bounce
cus-tom tail-ored vet — Asks me out for some-thing wet, — When the
asked to have a meal — By a big ty-coon in steel, — If the
Br.
Gtr.
Pno.
p
Cls., B. Cl.
vet be-gins to pet, — I cry "hoo-ray!" —
meal in-cludes a deal, — ac-cept I may! — But I'm
+ Br.
+ Hn.
mf
Vlns.
p
26
al-ways true to you, — dar-lin', in my fash-ion, Yes, I'm
2 Cls., Vla., Cello
Cls.
Br., W. W.
f
Str.
Cls.
p
al-ways true to you, — dar-lin' in my way. — I en-
I could
Cls.
+ Br., Hn.
Cym. short

34
joy a ten - der pass — By the boss of Bos - ton Mass. Though his
nev - er curl my lip — To a dazz - lin' dia - mond clip, Though the
Br.
Gtr.
Pno.
p
Cls., B. Cl.
pass is mid - dle class — and not "Back Bay!"
clip meant "let 'er rip" — I'd not say "Nay!"
But I'm
+ Br.
+ Hn.
mf
Vlns.
p
42
al - ways true to you, dar - lin', in my fash - ion.
Yes, I'm
Br., W. W.
2 Cls., Vla., Cello
Cls.
f
Str.
Cls.
p
al - ways true to you, — dar - lin', in my way. —
There's a
There's an
Cls.
Cymb.
Cls.
+ Br., Hn.

50
mad-man known as "Mack"_ Who is plan-ning to at - tack,_ If his
oil man known as "Tex"_ Who is keen to give me checks_ And his
Str. div.
Br.
mad at-tack_ means a Cad-il-lac,_ O - kay!
checks I fear,_ mean that Tex is here_ to stay! But I'm
+ Cl.
Br., W. W.
Str., Cls.
Cls., Pno.
58
al - ways true to you,_ dar - lin', in my fash - ion, Yes, I'm
pp dolce
f
Tutti
Br., Str. 8va
L. H.
subito p
+ Hn.
1.
al - ways true to you,_ dar-lin', in my way._ 2. I've been
Str.
Br., W. W.
+ Cls.
fp
ff

No.17a

1st Encore

Always True To You In My Fashion

Segue after applause

priest goes too far East, — I al-so stray. —
But I'm
+ Br.
Vlns.
+ Hn.
mf
p
13
al-ways true to you, — dar-lin', in my fash-ion,
Yes, I'm
Br., W. W.
Str.
2 Cls., Vla.
Cello
Cls.
f
p
al-ways true to you, — dar-lin', in my way. —
There's a
Cls.
+Br., Hn.
Cymb.
21
lush from Port-land, Ore. —
Who is rich but sich a bore.
When the
Br.
Gtr.
Pno.
Cls., B. Cl.

bore falls on the floor, I let him lay. But I'm
+ Br.
+ Hn.
mf
Vlns.
p
29
al - ways true to you, dar - lin', in my fash - ion, Yes, I'm
Br., W. W.
2 Cls., Vla., Cello
Cls.
f
Cls.
Str.
p
al - ways true to you, dar - lin', in my way. Mis - ter
Cls.
+Br., Hn.
Cym.
37
Har - ris, plu - to - crat Wants to give my cheek a pat, If the
Str. div.
Br.

Segue after applause

No.17b

2nd Encore
Always True To You In My Fashion

al - ways true to you, dar - lin', in my way.
There is
Cls.
+Br., Hn.
Cymb.
21
al - so Mis - ter Blotch, He's a whis - key king top - notch, Mis - ter
Br.
Br.
p
Gtr.
Pno.
Cls., B. Cl.
Blotch is full of Scotch and full of play.
But I'm
+ Br.
+ Hn.
mf
Vlns.
p
29
al - ways true to you, dar - lin', in my fash - ion,
Yes, I'm
Br., W. W.
Str.
2 Cls., Vla., Cello
Cls.
f
Cls.
p

Segue after applause

No.17c

Change Of Scene
(Why Can't You Behave?)

No.18 Bianca

Cue: FRED: You bore me.

GIRLS:
17
(laughing)
For your Bi - an - ca! Ha, ha, ha, ha, ha,
8va Str. pizz.
Cymb.
Br. (cups)
W. W., Hn.
Hn., B. Cl.
fp
2nd MESSENGER BOY:
Pack-age for Miss Lo-is Lane.
GIRLS:
For your Bi - an - ca!
Cls.
p
arco Str.
Hn., B. Cl.
33
3rd MESSENGER BOY: (Chauffeur)
Ha, ha, ha, ha, ha, Pack-age for Miss Lo-is Lane.
+ Str. pizz.
Br.
Cymb.
mf
Cello
più agitato
etc.
(Cello cont.)
4th MESSENGER BOY: (Banker)
Pack-age for Miss Lo-is Lane.
Str.
etc.
Cls.
Cls.

41 5th MESSENGER BOY: (Truckman)
GIRLS:
Pack - age for Miss Lo - is Lane. Ha, ha,
W. W.
etc.
(stacc.)
Hn., Cello Cls.
+ Trb.
f
ha, ha, ha, ha, ha. Ha, ha, ha, ha, ha, ha, ha. Your Bi - an - ca.
Str. 8va
W. W.
BILL: Suddenly slow
53 Allegretto
Ha! Sweet Bi - an - ca. While re - hears-ing with Bi - an - ca, She's the
Hp.
Vlns.
+Br.
Str.
p
Hn., Vla.
(Bs. tacet)
Bs.
+ Hp.
Cello pizz.
dar - ling I a - dore. Off stage, I found, She's been a - round, But I
+ Ob.
Cls.
Cls.
p
B. Cl.
(Str. out)

61 Allegretto
still love her more and more; So I've writ - ten her a love song, Though I'm
Str. div.
mf
p
Vla.
(W. W. tacet)
just an a - ma - teur, I'll sing it through for all of you, To
+Ob.
Str.
8va
(loco)
Cls.
+ Hp.
+ B. Cl.
see if it's wor-thy of her. Are you list - 'nin'? Bi -
Soft Shoe tempo
+ Br.
+ Hn.
p + Trb., B. Cl.
Bs.
+ Dr.
71
(GIRLS whistle) + Bells
(GIRLS whistle)
an - ca, Bi - an - ca, Oh,
Vlns.
Cls.
Br. div.
Vla., Cello

Br.
(GIRLS whistle)
79
ba - by, will you be mine? Bi - an - ca,
legato
Cls.
Vlns.
Br. div.
(GIRLS whistle)
Bi - an - ca, You'd bet - ter an - swer
Cls.
Vlns.
Cls.
87
(GIRLS whistle)
(+ Bells)
yes Or pop - pa span - ka. To win you,
Br.
mf
f
Br., Str.
p
Cls.
Vlns.
(GIRLS whistle)
Bi - an - ca, There's noth-ing I would not
Cls.
Vlns.
legato

Br.
do, I would swim from here to far Cas - a -
Str.
Hn.
blan - ca, Sweet Bi - an - ca, Bi - an - ca, For you.
Str.
Br. 8 bassa
+ Cls.
Cls.
mp
Hn., Cello
Str.
+ Br.
103
BILL: sings and dances
Bi - an - ca, Bi - an - ca, Oh,
SOPS.
Bi - an - ca, Bi - an - ca, Oh,
Fl., Picc.
ALTOS
Str.
Br., Cls.
Vlns.
Br.
Str.

baby, will you be mine?
Bi-
baby, will you be mine?
mine doodle-ooh doodle-ooh doo? Bi-
3
Str.
Cello
111
ff
mf
an-ca, Bi-an-ca! You'd better answer
an-ca, Bi-an-ca! You'd better answer
Br.
Str.
Cls.
119
yes Or poppa spanka. To win you,
yes Or poppa spanka. Radoo rahdoo-doo To win you,
Tpts.
Cymb.
Cello, Hns. Trb.
Fl., Picc.

Bi - an - ca, There's noth - ing I would not
Bi - an - ca, There's noth - ing I would not
R. H.
Trb., Cello, Hn.
127
do, I would glad - ly give up cof - fee for
do, I would glad - ly give up cof - fee for
Fl. Picc. + Vlns.
Br.
Br.
pp
San - ka, E - ven San - ka, Bi - an - ca, For you.
San - ka, E - ven San - ka, Bi - an - ca, For you.
Hn.
Saxs. 8 bassa
f

135
DANCE
Str., Hp. div.
Saxs.
+Br.
mp
Br., Cello, Bar.
Str.
Saxs.
Saxs.
143
Br.
Str. 8va
(+ Saxs. sust.)
Cello
151
Saxs.
Cymb.
Tutti
Br.
Saxs.
Saxs.
Br.
Saxs.
(Vlns. 8va)
Hn.
Br. open
Hn.

No.18a Incidental Music

Lilli - you can't walk out on me now

Cue: FRED: A spark of affection---a glimmer of love--

No.19 So In Love–Reprise

Cue: DOORMAN: Your cab's waiting, Miss Vanessi.

18
E - ven with - out you My arms fold
Str. (+ Cl. sust.)
+Cls.
26
a - bout you, You know dar - ling
W. W.
Br.
why, So in love with you am
Hn.
Fl.
Più mosso
(with freedom)
34
I. In love with the night mys - te - ri - ous,
Fl., E. H. soli
Hn.
Cls.
Str.
Str.

Tpt. Solo
The night when you first were there, In
Cls.
Hn. Solo
Fl., E. H.
42
Br., Hn. fp
love with my joy de - li - ri - ous When I
Cls.
(+ Timp.)
Tempo I°
50
knew that you could care. So taunt me
Br.
sfz
Str. unis.
pp
Fl., Cl.
(+ Cymb.)
+ B. Cl.
(B. Cl. sust.)
Bells
and hurt me, De - ceive me, de -
(Fl., Cl. cont.)
3
+ B. Cl.

58 Appassionato
sert me, I'm yours 'till I die,
W. W., Str. 8va
+ Hn.
mf
+ Br.
Hp.
Hn.
f
W. W.
So in love, So in love,
dim.
Br.
Str.
sfz
p
Fl., Ob.
(Str., B. Cl. sust.)
B. Cl.
Bell
So in love with you, my love, am
Cl.
70
I.
+ Str.
(Celesta) (W. W. cued)
Hp., Bells
Hp.
attacca

No.19a Change of Scene

Cut

No.20 Brush Up Your Shakespeare

Cue: 2nd GANGSTER: It's a boy.

29
Aes-chy-lus and Eu-ri-pi-des. One must know Hom-er, and
+Fl.
Str., Pno.
b'lieve me, bo, Soph-o-cles, al-so Sap-pho-ho. Un-
Cl., Fl., Str.
+ Cls.
+ Bsn., Cello
Fl. Bsn.
37
less you know Shell-ey and Keats and Pope, Dain-ty deb-bies will
45
call you a dope. But the po-et of them all, Who will
Fl.
Ob.
(Hp., Cls. sust.)
Str.
Cello, Bsn.
Fl.
tr

53
start 'em simply ravin', Is the poet people
tr
Ob.
3
sfz
call "The bard of Strat-ford-on-A-von."
Fl., Hp.
7
3 Solo Vlns.
f
Tutti
sf
8...:
61 Play 3 times
(BOTH) Brush up your Shake-speare, Start quot-ing him
(BOTH) Brush up your Shake-speare, Start quot-ing him
(BOTH) Brush up your Shake-speare, Start quot-ing him
Fl., Cl.
mf
Cello, Bsn.
Str.
69
now. Brush up your Shake-speare and the wom-en
now. Brush up your Shake-speare and the wom-en
now. Brush up your Shake-speare and the wom-en
W.W.div
Hp.

77
you will wow. (2nd G.) Just de - claim a few lines from O - thel - la
you will wow. (1st G.) With the wife of the Brit - ish Em - bessi - da
you will wow. (2nd G.) If you can't be a ham and do Ham - let,
Col. 8va
85
And they'll think you're a hell - uv - a fel - la, (1st G.) If your blonde won't re -
Try a crack out of Troi-lus and Cressi-da, (2nd G.) If she says she won't
They will not give a damn or a damn- let, (1st G.) Just re - cite an oc -
Fl.
Cls., Vln., Cello
Fl., Hp.
spond when you flat - ter 'er, Tell her what To - ny told Cle - o - pat-er-er. (2nd G.) If she
buy it or tike — it, Make her tike it, what's more, As You Like It. (BOTH) If she
cas - sion-al son - net, And your lap 'll have "Hon-ey" up - on it. (2nd G.) When your
Ob., Vln.
Cls.
93
fights when her clothes you are muss - ing, (BOTH) What are clothes? Much A -
says your be - hav - ior is hein - ous, Kick her right in the
ba - by is plead - ing for pleas - ure, (BOTH) Let her sam - ple your
Fl.
Str., W.W.

101
do A-bout Nuss-ing.
Cor-i-o-la-nus.
Meas-ure for Meas-ure.
Brush up your Shake-speare
Brush up your Shake-speare
Brush up your Shake-speare
Fl., Cl.
Ob., Vln.
etc.
Hp.
f Tutti
Str.
Cello, Bsn.
1.2.
And they'll all kow - tow.
And they'll all kow - tow.
And they'll all kow -
Fl., Cl.
Br., Str. 8va
f Tutti
mf
3.
tow For-sooth, And they'll all
Str., Ob., Bsn.
kow - tow. I' faith, And they'll all kow - tow.
Tutti
attacca

No.20a

First Encore
Brush Up Your Shakespeare

1st:
25
Bet - ter men - tion the Mer - chant of Ven - ice When her
col 8va
sweet pound o' flesh you would men - ace.
2nd:
33
Fl.
If her vir - tue, at
Cls., Vln., Cello
first, she de - fends, well, Just re - mind her that All's well that
Vln., Ob.
Cls.
ends well.
1st:
41
And if still she won't give you a bon - us,
Fl., Hp.
Str., W. W.
Fl.

BOTH:
You know what Ven - us got from A - don - is!
mf
Hp.
f Tutti
49
Brush up your Shake - speare And they'll all
Fl., Cl.
p
Cello Bsn.
57
kow - tow. Thinks thou, and they'll all kow -
Str., Ob.
+ Bsn.
tow. Odds bod - kins, They'll all kow - tow.
Tutti
f
8...:

Second Encore

No.20b Brush Up Your Shakespeare

2nd:
And the wom - en you will wow. If your
col 8va
25
goil is a Wash - ing - ton heights dream, Treat the kid to A
1st:
33
Mid - sum - mer's Night's Dream. If she then wants an all - by - her-
Cls., Vln., Cello
self night, Let her rest ev - 'ry 'lev - enth or Twelf Night.
Vln., Ob.
Cls.
Fl., Hp.

BOTH:
41
If be - cause of your heat she gets huf - fy, Sim - ply
Str., W. W.
Fl.
49
play on and "Lay on, Mac - duf - fy!" Brush
Fl., Cl.
mf
Hp.
f Tutti
p
Cello Bsn.
up your Shake - speare And they'll all kow -
tow! We trow, And they'll all kow - tow.
f Tutti
attacca

No.21

Pavane
(Why Can't You Behave?)

Vln. 1
(Ob., Vln. 2)
Vla., Cello
Hn.
(Hp., Pno.)
Ob., Vlns.
Cl., Hp.
Vla., Cello
Vln. 1, Cl.
(Cls., Vln 2)
Hn., Vla.
+ Ob.
R. H.
Fl.
etc.
(+ Tpt. 1)
(+ Trb.)
tr
+ Hn.
rit.
attacca

No.22 I Am Ashamed That Women Are So Simple

Cue: PETRUCHIO: Duty they do owe to their lords and husbands.

Andantino
KATHERINE: with calm diction, almost solemnly
I am a-shamed that wom-en are so sim-ple — To
Str., W. W.
p molto legato
+ Hn.
+ Bs.
of-fer war where they should kneel for peace. Or seek for rule, su-pre-ma-cy and
sway, When they are bound to serve, love, and o-bey. Why
p
dolce
10
are our bod-ies soft and weak and smooth, Un-apt to toil and trou-ble in the
W. W.
Str., Hp., Celesta
pp
Solo Cello
Str., Hp.

world. But that our soft con - di - tions and our hearts Should well a -
+ Bsn.
+ Hn.
Hn.
Cello
gree with our ex - ter - nal parts? So wife, hold your tem - per and
18 Broader, with great emphasis
3
mf Tutti
+ Hn.
subito p
+ Cello, Bsn.
+ Trb.
Timp.
meek - ly put Your hand 'neath the sole of your hus - band's foot, In
f Tutti
Str., W. W.
poco rit.
to - ken of which du - ty, if he please, My hand is read - y,
p
f
Str.
Tpts.
Str.
Br.
Timp.
W. W.
Hp.
Bsn.
Cello, Hn.

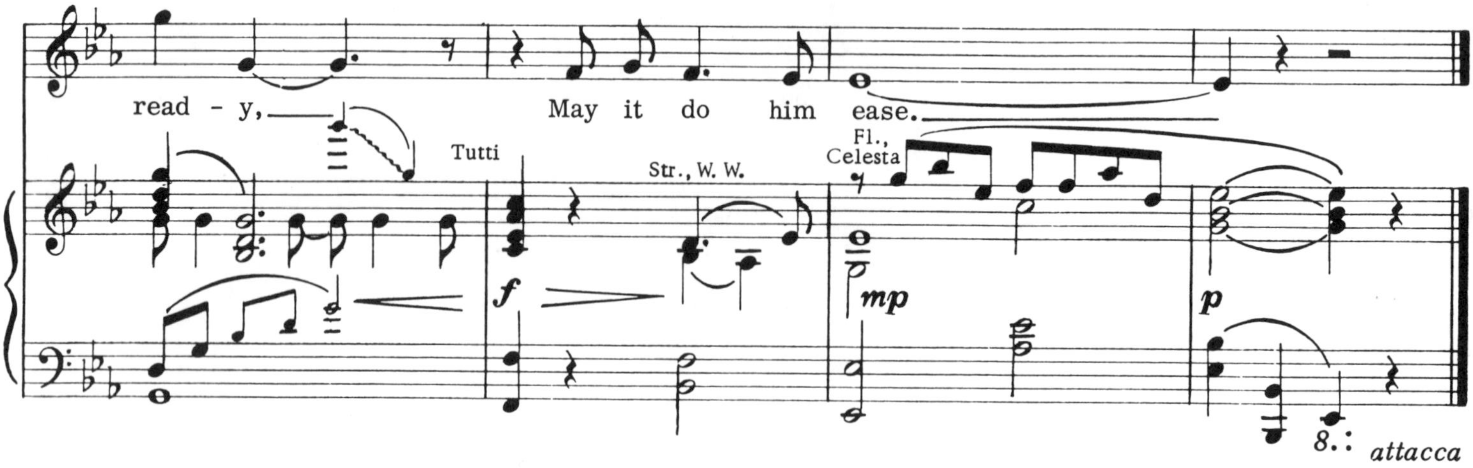

No.23

Shrew Finale
So Kiss Me, Kate

Cue: PETRUCHIO: Come on and kiss me, Kate.

Car - o! Car - iss - i - mo!
And twice and thrice, Ere we start
Bel - lo! Bel - liss - i - mo!
Liv - ing in Par - a - dise, Oh,
Oh,
Oh,
Oh,
cresc.

Cl.
ff
Pres - to! Pres - tiss - i mo!
kiss me, Kate, Darling angel, divine! For
kiss me, Kate, Darling angel, divine!
W. W.
kiss me, Kate, Darling angel, divine!
kiss me, Kate, Darling angel, divine!
W. W., Hn., Br., colla voce)
Str., Pno., Hp., Gtr.
f
15 Fast Waltz - in 1
Now thou shall ever be
now thou shall ever be
mf
Now thou shall
mf
Now thou shall
mf
Now thou shall
15 Fast Waltz - in 1
(Str., W. W., Hn. colla voce)
p
(Br. sust.)
mf

23
+ Fl., Ob.
Now thou shall ever be Mine,
+ Vlns.
ever be Mine,
Now thou shall ever be
ever be
ever be
pp Cello, Bsn.
Darling, mine, And I am thine, and I am
Darling, mine, And I am thine, and I am
cresc.
poco allarg.
And she is thine, and she is
Fl., Ob., Vlns.
+ Br.

No.24 Finale-Dance

tr
9
tr
tr
+ 8va
tr
tr
+ 8va
17
tr
tr
tr
tr
25

col 8va
33
col 8va
Hp.
+ Timp.
37
41
W. W., Str.
Br., Pno.
tr
tr
Br., Pno.
45
Tutti
cresc.
(CURTAIN)
fz p
attacca

No.24a Grand Finale-Last Curtain

21
KATHERINE & PETRUCHIO:
So to - night just re - cite to your ma - tie. Kiss me,
Str., W. W. (cued in Br.)
Hp.
Kate, Kiss me, Kate, Kiss me, Ka - tie.
29 ALL:
Brush
(+8va)
mf
mf
up your Shake - speare And they'll all
kow - tow.
Unis. Tutti

END OF ACT II